T R E A T S

just great recipes

GENERAL INFORMATION

The level of difficulty of the recipes in this book
is expressed as a number from 1 (simple) to 3 (difficult).

TREATS
just great recipes
pizza

M^cRAE BOOKS

Making Pizzas at Home

Making pizzas at home is both easy and fun. It also fits in well with busy schedules since the dough can be prepared ahead of time and many toppings only take a few minutes to prepare. Most children love to eat pizza; they will also enjoy helping to knead the dough and sprinkling it with cheese and herbs for the toppings.

The ingredients given in the basic pizza dough recipe will make about 1 pound (500 g) of dough. This is enough to make one large pizza, sufficient for 2–4 people.

SERVES 2–4

PREPARATION 20 min

RISING TIME about 1 h 30 min

DIFFICULTY level 1

Pizza Dough

Place the fresh or active dry yeast in a small bowl and add half the warm water. Stir gently until the yeast has dissolved. Set aside for 15 minutes. • Place the flour and salt in a large bowl. Pour in the yeast mixture and most of the remaining water and stir well. • Place the dough on a lightly floured work surface and knead gently and with the lightest possible touch until the dough is smooth and elastic, about 10 minutes. • Shape into a ball and place in a large oiled bowl. Set aside to rise until doubled in volume, about 1 hour 30 minutes.

1 oz (30 g) fresh yeast or 2 (¼-oz/7-g) packages active dry yeast

About ⅔ cup (150 ml) warm water

3 cups (450 g) all-purpose (plain) flour

½ teaspoon salt

Thickness of the dough

Some people like thick, doughy pizza crusts while others prefer them to be thin and crisp. In Italy, the thick, bread-like crusts are typical of pizzas made in Sicily and the south. Further north, crusts are thinner. Some pizzerias in Florence serve pizzas with such thin crusts that if you roll the topping up in them it is more like eating a crêpe than a pizza. Try several thicknesses, and decide which one you and your family prefer.

1 To shape the pizza with a rolling pin, roll the dough out into a disk of the desired thickness. To finish, use your fingertips to make a rim around the edge of the pizza so that the topping won't drip out during cooking. Transfer the dough to a pizza pan or oiled baking sheet.

3 When the pizza dough has been shaped and is in the pizza pan or on the baking sheet, set it aside for 10 minutes before adding the topping. This will give the dough time to regain some volume and will make the crust lighter and more appetizing.

2 To shape the pizza by hand, place the dough in the oiled pizza pan and push it outward with your fingertips, spreading it to fit the pan.

4–5 To make calzones, proceed as for pizza, giving the dough a round shape. Place the topping on one half of the dough only, leaving a 1-inch (2-5-cm) border around the edge. Fold the other half over the filling and press the edges together with your fingertips to seal.

SERVES 2–4
PREPARATION 30 min
RISING TIME about 1 h 30 min
COOKING 35 min
DIFFICULTY level 1

Pizza
with olives and anchovies

Prepare the pizza dough following the instructions on pages 4–5. Set aside to rise. • Preheat the oven to 425°F (220°C/gas 7). • Oil a 12-inch (30-cm) pizza pan. • Heat half the oil in a large frying pan over medium heat. Add the onion and garlic and sauté until transparent, 3–4 minutes. • Stir in the tomatoes, olives, and chile powder, if using, and season lightly with salt and pepper. Simmer over low heat until slightly reduced, about 10 minutes. • Knead the risen pizza dough briefly on a lightly floured work surface then press it into the prepared pan using your hands. • Spread the sauce over the dough. Arrange the anchovies on top and drizzle with the remaining oil. • Bake until the base is crisp and golden brown, about 20 minutes. • Serve hot or at room temperature.

1 lb (500 g) pizza dough (see page 4)
1/4 cup (60 ml) extra-virgin olive oil
1 clove garlic, finely chopped
1 small onion, finely chopped
1 (14-oz/400-g) canned tomatoes, chopped, with juice
1 cup (100 g) black olives, pitted
1/2 teaspoon chile powder (optional)
Salt and freshly ground black pepper
4 salted anchovies or 8 salted anchovy fillets, rinsed and coarsely chopped

SERVES 2–4
PREPARATION 30 min
RISING TIME about 1 h 30 min
COOKING 20–25 min
DIFFICULTY level 1

Pizza Margherita

Prepare the pizza dough following the instructions on pages 4–5. Set aside to rise. • Preheat the oven to 425°F (220°C/gas 7). • Oil a 12-inch (30-cm) pizza pan. • Knead the risen pizza dough briefly on a lightly floured work surface then press it into the prepared pan using your hands. • Spread the tomato over the dough and season with salt and pepper. Drizzle with half the oil. • Bake for 15 minutes. • Remove from the oven and top with mozzarella. Bake until the base is crisp and golden brown and the mozzarella has melted, 5–10 minutes. • Drizzle with the remaining oil and garnish with the basil. Serve hot or at room temperature.

1 lb (500 g) pizza dough (see page 4)
1 (14-oz/400-g) canned tomatoes, drained and chopped
Salt and freshly ground black pepper
5 oz (150 g) fresh mozzarella cheese, drained and chopped
2 tablespoons extra-virgin olive oil
Sprigs of fresh basil, to garnish

SERVES 2–4
PREPARATION 40 min
RISING TIME about 1 h 30 min
COOKING 35–40 min
DIFFICULTY level 1

Pizza
with onion and bell peppers

Prepare the pizza dough following the instructions on pages 4–5. Set aside to rise. • Preheat the oven to 425°F (220°C/gas 7). • Oil a 12-inch (30-cm) pizza pan. • Heat 3 tablespoons of oil in a large frying pan over medium heat. Add the onions and sauté until transparent, 3–4 minutes. • Add the bell peppers and sauté until softened, 7–10 minutes. Season with salt and pepper. • Knead the risen pizza dough briefly on a lightly floured work surface then press it into the prepared pan using your hands. • Spread the dough with the onion and bell pepper mixture. Top with the anchovies. Sprinkle with the olives and drizzle with the remaining oil. • Bake until the base is crisp and golden brown, about 20 minutes. • Garnish with the basil. Serve hot or at room temperature.

1 lb (500 g) pizza dough (see page 4)
1/4 cup (60 ml) extra-virgin olive oil
2 large onions, finely sliced
2 large red bell peppers (capsicums), seeded and thinly sliced
Salt and freshly ground black pepper
4–6 anchovy fillets, chopped
1/2 cup (50 g) black olives, pitted
Fresh basil leaves, to garnish

Pizza
with cherry tomatoes and oregano

Prepare the pizza dough following the instructions on pages 4–5. Incorporate the mashed potato and 2 tablespoons of oil into the dough as you knead. Set aside to rise. • Preheat the oven to 425°F (220°C/gas 7). • Oil a 12-inch (30-cm) pizza pan. • Knead the risen pizza dough briefly on a lightly floured work surface then press it into the prepared pan using your hands. • Place the tomatoes on the dough. Season with salt, pepper, and oregano. Drizzle with the remaining oil. • Bake until the base is crisp and golden brown, about 20 minutes. • Serve hot or at room temperature.

1 lb (500 g) pizza dough (see page 4)
1 large potato, boiled and mashed
1/4 cup (60 ml) extra-virgin olive oil
Salt and freshly ground black pepper
20 cherry tomatoes, thinly sliced
1 teaspoon dried oregano

SERVES 2–4
PREPARATION 30 min
RISING TIME about 1 h 30 min
COOKING 35 min
DIFFICULTY level 1

Rustic Pizza
with sausage and mushrooms

Prepare the pizza dough following the instructions on pages 4–5. Set aside to rise. • Preheat the oven to 425°F (220°C/gas 7). • Oil a 12-inch (30-cm) pizza pan. • Heat the oil in a large frying pan over medium heat. Add the onions and sauté until transparent, 3–4 minutes. • Add the sausage and mushrooms and sauté until the sausage is browned, about 5 minutes. Season with salt and pepper. • Knead the risen pizza dough briefly on a lightly floured work surface then press it into the prepared pan using your hands. • Spread the tomato over the dough. Add the onions, sausage, mushrooms, and mozzarella, spreading them as evenly as possible. • Bake until the base is crisp and golden brown, about 25 minutes. • Top with the cherry tomatoes and serve hot.

1 lb (500 g) pizza dough (see page 4)
2 tablespoons extra-virgin olive oil
2 small onions, thinly sliced
8 oz (250 g) Italian sausages, skinned and sliced
8 oz (250 g) button mushrooms, sliced
Salt and freshly ground black pepper
¾ cup (200 g) canned tomatoes, chopped, with juice
5 oz (150 g) fresh mozzarella, drained and thinly sliced
2–4 cherry tomatoes, cut in half

SERVES 2–4
PREPARATION 30 min
RISING TIME about 1 h 30 min
COOKING 45 min
DIFFICULTY level 2

Pizza
with ratatouille and green olives

Prepare the pizza dough following the instructions on pages 4–5. Set aside to rise. • Preheat the oven to 425°F (220°C/gas 7). • Oil a 12-inch (30-cm) pizza pan. • Place the chopped eggplant in a colander. Sprinkle with the salt and let rest for 30 minutes. • Rinse the eggplant and drain well. • Blanch the tomatoes in boiling water for 2 minutes. Drain and slip off the skins. Slice the tomatoes. • Heat 2 tablespoons of oil in a medium saucepan over medium heat. Add the onions, garlic, parsley, eggplant, bell peppers, tomato, and zucchini and simmer until tender, 15–20 minutes. Stir frequently during the cooking time. • Remove and discard the garlic. • Knead the risen pizza dough briefly on a lightly floured work surface then press it into the prepared pan using your hands. • Spread the ratatouille over the dough. Sprinkle with the olives. Season with salt and pepper. • Bake until the base is crisp and golden brown, about 25 minutes. • Sprinkle with the thyme and drizzle with the remaining oil. Serve hot.

1 lb (500 g) pizza dough (see page 4)
1 large eggplant, peeled and cut into small cubes
Salt
1 lb (500 g) ripe tomatoes
3 tablespoons extra-virgin olive oil
2 small onions, finely sliced
1 clove garlic, lightly crushed but whole
1 tablespoon finely chopped parsley
2 red bell peppers, (capsicums) seeded and finely sliced
3 small zucchini (courgettes), sliced
1/2 cup (50 g) large green olives, pitted
Freshly ground black pepper
1 tablespoon finely chopped thyme

SERVES 2–4	# Pizza
PREPARATION 30 min	
RISING TIME about 1 h 30 min	
COOKING 20–25 min	
DIFFICULTY level 1	## with spicy salami

Prepare the pizza dough following the instructions on pages 4–5. Set aside to rise. • Preheat the oven to 425°F (220°C/gas 7). • Oil a 12-inch (30-cm) pizza pan. • Knead the risen pizza dough briefly on a lightly floured work surface then press it into the prepared pan using your hands. • Spread the tomatoes over the dough. Cover with the salami and onion. Drizzle with the oil. • Bake for 15 minutes then add the mozzarella. Bake until the base is crisp and golden brown and the mozzarella has melted, 5–10 minutes. • Sprinkle with oregano and serve hot or at room temperature.

1 lb (500 g) pizza dough (see page 4)
1 (14-oz/440-g) can tomatoes, chopped, with juice
5 oz (150 g) fresh mozzarella cheese, drained and cut into small cubes
Salt
5 oz (150 g) spicy salami, thinly sliced
1 white onion, very thinly sliced
3 tablespoons extra-virgin olive oil
1 teaspoon dried oregano

Potato Pizza
with mushrooms

Cook the potatoes in a large pot of salted boiling water until tender, about 25 minutes. Mash half the potatoes and thinly slice the rest. • Prepare the pizza dough following the instructions on pages 4–5 incorporating the mashed potatoes and 2 tablespoons of oil into the dough as you knead. Set aside to rise for 2 hours. • Preheat the oven to 425°F (220°C/gas 7). • Oil a 12-inch (30-cm) pizza pan. • Heat 2 tablespoons of oil in a large frying pan over medium heat. Add the garlic and sauté until pale gold, 3 minutes. Add the mushrooms and sauté until tender, about 5 minutes. Season with salt and pepper. • Stir in the parsley and thyme. • Knead the risen pizza dough briefly on a lightly floured work surface then press it into the prepared pan using your hands. • Spread the sliced potatoes and mushrooms over the dough. Drizzle with the remaining oil. • Bake for 15 minutes then add the mozzarella. Bake until the base is crisp and golden brown and the mozzarella is melted, 5–10 minutes. • Serve hot.

1 lb (500 g) potatoes, peeled
1 lb (500 g) pizza dough (see page 4)
½ cup (125 ml) extra-virgin olive oil
1 clove garlic, finely chopped
8 oz (250 g) white mushrooms, sliced
Salt and freshly ground black pepper
1 tablespoon freshly chopped parsley
1 tablespoon freshly chopped thyme
4 oz (125 g) fresh mozzarella cheese, drained and sliced thinly

SERVES 4
PREPARATION 1 h
RISING TIME about 2 h
COOKING 15–20 min
DIFFICULTY level 3

Puffy Pizza
with artichokes and pancetta

Prepare the pizza dough following the instructions on pages 4–5. Set aside to rise. • Oil a 14-inch (35-cm) pizza pan. • Remove the tough outer leaves from the artichokes. Cut off the top third of the leaves. Cut in half and scrape out any fuzzy inner core. Slice finely. Place in a bowl of water with the lemon juice. • Roll out the pizza dough on a lightly floured surface to make a 10 inch (25 cm) disk. Put the puff pastry in the center and wrap the pizza dough around it. Roll out on a lightly floured surface to make a 5 x 14-inch (13 x 35-cm) strip . Fold the ends in toward the center. Roll out again to the same size as before. Fold the ends of the strip in again and repeat the process. Chill for 20 minutes. Repeat the rolling and folding process again three times. Chill for another 20 minutes. • Preheat the oven to 425°F (220°C/gas 7). • Roll the dough out again. Repeat the folding process, then roll out into a 14-inch (35-cm) disk and place in the prepared pizza pan. • Season with salt and drizzle with 2 tablespoons of the oil. • Bake until golden brown and cooked through, 15–20 minutes. Remove from the oven and keep warm. • Heat 1 tablespoon of the oil in a small frying pan over medium heat. Add the pancetta and prosciutto and sauté until lightly browned and crisp, about 5 minutes. • Drain the artichokes. Heat 2 tablespoons of the oil in a large frying pan over medium heat. Add the artichokes, garlic, and wine. Simmer until the artichokes are tender, 10–15 minutes. • Heat the remaining oil in a small frying pan over medium heat. Add the onion and sauté until tender, 5 minutes. Add the sugar, cover, and simmer over low heat until the onion is lightly browned and slightly caramelized, 10–15 minutes. • Spread the base with the onion mixture and top with the artichokes and prosciutto mixture. Serve hot.

1 lb (500 g) pizza dough (see page 4)
4 artichokes
Juice of 1/2 a lemon
4 oz (125 g) frozen puff pastry, thawed
Salt
1/3 cup (90 ml) extra-virgin olive oil
3 oz (90 g) pancetta, chopped
2 oz (60 g) prosciutto (Parma ham), chopped
1 clove garlic, finely chopped
2 tablespoons dry white wine
1 large onion, thinly sliced
1 teaspoon sugar

SERVES 2–4
PREPARATION 45 min
RISING TIME about 1 h 30 min
COOKING 35 min
DIFFICULTY level 1

Pizza
with zucchini and egg

Prepare the pizza dough following the instructions on pages 4–5. Set aside to rise. • Preheat the oven to 425°F (220°C/gas 7). • Oil two baking sheets. • Heat 2 tablespoons of oil in a large frying pan over medium heat. Add the onion and zucchini. Sauté until tender, 5–7 minutes. • Season with salt and pepper and remove from the heat. • Divide the dough into 4 portions. Roll out the pieces of dough on a lightly floured work surface to make four ½-inch (1-cm) thick disks. Transfer to the baking sheets. • Spread each disk with some of the tomatoes and zucchini mixture. Drizzle with the remaining oil. • Bake for 10 minutes. Remove from the oven and break an egg onto each pizza. Sprinkle each one with mozzarella. Season with salt and pepper. Bake until the egg is cooked and the pizza crust is crisp and golden brown, 10–15 minutes. • Serve hot.

1 lb (500 g) pizza dough (see page 4)
¼ cup (60 ml) extra-virgin olive oil
1 large onion, thinly sliced
8 oz (250 g) zucchini (courgettes), thinly sliced
Salt and freshly ground black pepper
8 oz (250 g) tomatoes, peeled and thinly sliced
4 eggs
4 oz (125 g) fresh mozzarella cheese, drained and sliced thinly

Pizza
with spinach and egg

Prepare the pizza dough following the instructions on pages 4–5. Set aside to rise. • Preheat the oven to 400°F (200°C/gas 6). • Oil two baking sheets. • Melt the butter in a large frying pan over medium heat. Add the spinach and sauté for 2–3 minutes. Remove from the heat. Divide the dough into 4 portions. Roll out the pieces of dough on a lightly floured work surface to make four $^1/_2$-inch (1-cm) thick disks. Transfer to the baking sheets. • Spread some of the chopped tomato over each disk and season with salt and pepper. Cover with the spinach, ham, and mozzarella. • Bake for 10 minutes. Remove from the oven and break an egg onto each pizza. Season with a little more salt and pepper. Sprinkle with Parmesan. • Bake until the egg is cooked and the pizza crust is crisp and golden brown, 10–15 minutes. • Serve hot.

1 lb (500 g) pizza dough (see page 4)
8 oz (250 g) ripe tomatoes, peeled and chopped
2 tablespoons butter
12 oz (350 g) cooked spinach, drained
Salt and freshly ground black pepper
5 oz (150 g) ham, chopped
5 oz (150 g) fresh mozzarella cheese, drained and thinly sliced
4 large eggs
$^3/_4$ cup (100 g) freshly grated Parmesan

SERVES 2–4
PREPARATION 30 min
RISING TIME about 1 h 30 min
COOKING 20–25 min
DIFFICULTY level 1

Red Pizza
with onion and pesto

Prepare the pizza dough following the instructions on pages 4–5. Set aside to rise. • Preheat the oven to 425°F (220°C/gas 7). • Oil two 8-inch (20-cm) pizza pans. • Pesto: Chop the basil and garlic with a pinch of salt in a food processor. Add the pine nuts, Parmesan, and Pecorino and chop until smooth. Stir the oil in by hand. The pesto should be smooth and fairly dense. • Roll out the pizza dough on a lightly floured work surface into two 8-inch (20-cm) disks, Place in the prepared pans. • Spread evenly with the tomatoes. Season with salt. • Bake for 10 minutes. Remove from the oven and add the onions, sprinkling them evenly over the two pizzas. • Bake for until the base is crisp and the onions are lightly browned, 10–15 minutes. Remove from the oven and dot with the pesto. • Serve hot.

1 lb (500 g) pizza dough (see page 4)

Pesto
1 large bunch of basil
2 cloves garlic
Salt
2 tablespoons pine nuts
2 tablespoons freshly grated Parmesan cheese
2 tablespoons freshly grated Pecorino cheese
1/2 cup (125 ml) extra-virgin olive oil

1 (14-oz/400-g) can tomatoes, chopped, with juice
Salt
4 small white onions, finely sliced

SERVES 2–4
PREPARATION 45 min
RISING TIME about 1 h 30 min
COOKING 20–25 min
DIFFICULTY level 1

Pizza
with bell peppers

Prepare the pizza dough following the instructions on pages 4–5. Set aside to rise. • Preheat the oven to 400°F (200°C/gas 6). • Oil a 12-inch (30-cm) pizza pan. • Place the risen dough on a lightly floured work surface and, gradually incorporating 3 tablespoons of the oil, knead until the dough is smooth and the oil is well incorporated, 10–15 minutes. • Press the dough into the prepared pan using your hands. • Spread the tomatoes evenly over the dough. Top with the onions, bell peppers, garlic, and basil. Season with salt and pepper. Drizzle with the remaining oil. • Bake until the topping is cooked and the base is crisp and golden brown, 20–25 minutes. • Serve hot or at room temperature.

1 lb (500 g) pizza dough (see page 4)
12 oz (350 g) ripe tomatoes, peeled and thinly sliced
1/4 cup (60 ml) extra-virgin olive oil
2 small white onions, finely sliced
1 large yellow bell pepper (capsicum), seeded and thinly sliced
1 large red bell pepper (capsicum), seeded and thinly sliced
2 cloves garlic, finely chopped
2 tablespoons finely chopped basil
Salt and freshly ground black pepper

SERVES 2–4
PREPARATION 1 h
RISING TIME about 1 h 30 min
COOKING 25–30 min
DIFFICULTY level 1

Pizza
with eggplant and tomatoes

Prepare the pizza dough following the instructions on pages 4–5. Set aside to rise. • Oil a 12-inch (30-cm) pizza pan. • Put the eggplant into a colander and sprinkle with salt. Let rest for 10 minutes. Rinse and drain well. Arrange the eggplant on a plate. Drizzle with half the oil. Sprinkle with the red pepper flakes and the garlic. Let rest for 30 minutes. • Preheat the oven to 400°F (200°C/gas 6). • Preheat a grill pan or griddle over high heat. Cook the eggplant until tender, about 5 minutes each side. • Knead the risen pizza dough briefly on a lightly floured work surface then press it into the prepared pan using your hands. • Spread with the canned tomatoes. Season with salt. Add the eggplant and olives and drizzle with the remaining oil. Bake for 15 minutes. • Add the mozzarella and bake until the base is crisp and golden brown, 5–10 minutes. • Top with the cherry tomatoes and serve hot.

1 lb (500 g) pizza dough (see page 4)
1 large eggplant (aubergine), thinly sliced
Salt
1/3 cup (90 ml) extra-virgin olive oil
1/2 teaspoon red pepper flakes
1 clove garlic, finely chopped
1 cup (250 g) canned tomatoes, chopped, with juice
5 oz (150 g) fresh mozzarella cheese, drained and sliced thinly
Handful of black olives, pitted
8 oz (250 g) cherry tomatoes, sliced

SERVES 2–4
PREPARATION 30 min
RISING TIME about 1 h 30 min
COOKING 20–25 min
DIFFICULTY level 1

Pizza
with apple and gorgonzola

Prepare the pizza dough following the instructions on pages 4–5. Set aside to rise. • Preheat the oven to 425°F (220°C/gas 7). • Oil a 12-inch (30-cm) pizza pan. • Mash the Gorgonzola in a bowl using a fork until smooth and creamy. • Add the apples to the Gorgonzola. Mix well. • Knead the risen pizza dough briefly on a lightly floured work surface then press it into the prepared pan using your hands. • Cover the dough with slices of mozzarella. Spread with the Gorgonzola and apple mixture. Season with salt and pepper. Drizzle with the oil.• Bake until the topping is lightly browned and the base is crisp and golden brown. • Garnish with coriander and serve hot.

1 lb (500 g) pizza dough (see page 4)

8 oz (250 g) Gorgonzola cheese,
at room temperature

2 ripe Granny Smith apples, peeled,
cored, and thinly sliced

4 oz (125 g) fresh mozzarella, drained
and sliced thinly

Salt and freshly ground black pepper

2 tablespoons extra-virgin olive oil

Sprigs of coriander, to garnish

25

SERVES 2–4
PREPARATION 45 min
RISING TIME about 1 h 30 min
COOKING 45–50 min
DIFFICULTY level 1

Pizza
with ground beef and onions

Prepare the pizza dough following the instructions on pages 4–5. Set aside to rise. • Oil a 12-inch (30-cm) pizza pan. • Heat 2 tablespoons of the oil in a large frying pan over medium heat. Add the onions and sauté until transparent, 3–4 minutes. • Add 1 tablespoon of water and simmer until the onions are tender, 2 minutes. Set aside. • Add the tomatoes and basil to the pan and sauté for 1 minute over high heat. Season with salt and pepper. Sauté until the tomatoes begin to break down, 10 minutes. Set aside. • Heat 2 tablespoons of oil in the pan over high heat. Add the meat and sauté until browned. 5–7 minutes. • Add the stock and season with salt and pepper. Lower the heat and simmer until the meat is cooked and most of the liquid has evaporated, 15 minutes. • Preheat the oven to 425°F (220°C/gas 7). • Stir the tomatoes into the meat. • Knead the risen pizza dough briefly on a lightly floured work surface then press it into the prepared pan using your hands. • Spread with the meat and tomato mixture. Top with the onions. Drizzle with the remaining oil, • Bake until the base is crisp and golden brown. • Serve hot.

1 lb (500 g) pizza dough (see page 4)
1/4 cup (60 ml) extra-virgin olive oil
2 medium onions, finely sliced
4 large ripe tomatoes, sliced
2 tablespoons finely chopped basil
Salt and freshly ground black pepper
12 oz (350 g) lean minced beef
1/3 cup (90 ml) beef stock

SERVES 2–4
PREPARATION 30 min
RISING TIME about 1 h 30 min
COOKING 20–25 min
DIFFICULTY level 1

Spicy Pizza
with salami and black olives

Prepare the pizza dough following the instructions on pages 4–5. Set aside to rise. • Preheat the oven to 400°F (200°C/gas 6). • Oil an 8 x 12-inch (20 x 30-cm) rectangular pizza pan. • Knead the risen pizza dough briefly on a lightly floured work surface then press it into the prepared pan using your hands. • Arrange the salami, olives, tomatoes, and onions on top of the dough. Season with salt and pepper. Drizzle with the oil and sprinkle with oregano. • Bake until the topping is cooked and the base is crisp and golden brown, 20–25 minutes. • Serve hot.

1 lb (500 g) pizza dough (see page 4)
6 oz (180 g) spicy salami, thinly sliced
12 black olives, pitted
10 cherry tomatoes, sliced
4 baby onions, thinly sliced
Salt and freshly ground black pepper
$1/4$ cup (60 ml) extra-virgin olive oil
1 teaspoon dried oregano

SERVES 2–4
PREPARATION 30 min
RISING TIME about 1 h 30 min
COOKING 10–15 min
DIFFICULTY level 1

Little Pizzas
with herbs and cream cheese

Prepare the pizza dough following the instructions on pages 4–5, incorporating the herbs into the dough as you work. Set aside to rise. • Preheat the oven to 400°F (200°C/gas 6). • Oil two baking sheets. • Knead the risen dough on a lightly floured work surface for 1 minute then roll out to ¼ inch (5 mm) thick. Cut into 2½-inch (7-cm) disks using a cookie cutter. Brush each disk with a little of the oil. • Arrange the disks on the prepared baking sheets. Season with salt and bake until crisp and golden browned, 10–15 minutes. Remove from the oven and let cool slightly. • Spread each pizza with a little of the cream cheese. Garnish with sprigs of fresh herbs. • Serve war or at room temperature.

1 lb (500 g) pizza dough (see page 4)
1 tablespoon finely chopped parsley.
  + sprigs to garnish
1 tablespoon finely chopped rosemary.
  + sprigs to garnish
1 tablespoon finely chopped marjoram.
  + sprigs to garnish
1 tablespoon finely chopped thyme.
  + sprigs to garnish
1 tablespoon finely chopped basil.
  + sprigs to garnish
¼ cup (60 ml) extra-virgin olive oil
Salt
8 oz (250 g) cream cheese

SERVES 2–4
PREPARATION 40 min
RISING TIME about 1 h 30 min
COOKING 40 min
DIFFICULTY level 1

Pizza
with tuna and peas

Prepare the pizza dough following the instructions on pages 4–5. Set aside to rise. • Preheat the oven to 425°F (220°C/gas 7). • Oil a 14-inch (35-cm) pizza pan. • Heat half the oil in a large frying pan over medium heat. Add the onion and sauté until transparent, 3–4 minutes. • Add the tomatoes and simmer for 10 minutes. • Stir in the tuna and peas and simmer for 2 minutes. • Knead the risen pizza dough briefly on a lightly floured work surface then press it into the pan using your hands. • Spread with the tomato mixture. Sprinkle with capers and drizzle with the remaining oil. • Bake for 15 minutes. Top with the mozzarella and season with salt and pepper. Bake until the base is crisp and golden brown and the mozzarella is melted, 5–10 minutes. • Serve hot.

1 lb (500 g) pizza dough (see page 4)
¼ cup (60 ml) extra-virgin olive oil
1 large onion, sliced
Salt
1 (14-oz/400-g) can tomatoes, chopped, with juice
5 oz (150 g) canned tuna, drained and crumbled
1 cup (150 g) frozen peas
1 tablespoon capers preserved in brine, drained
4 oz (125 g) fresh mozzarella, drained and sliced thinly
Freshly ground black pepper

Pizza
with onion, cheese, and walnuts

Prepare the pizza dough following the instructions on pages 4–5. Set aside to rise. • Preheat the oven to 425°F (220°C/gas 7). • Oil a 12-inch (30-cm) pizza pan. • Mix the Gorgonzola in a bowl using a fork, until it is smooth and creamy. Stir in the Worchestershire sauce. • Knead the risen pizza dough briefly on a lightly floured work surface then press it into the prepared pan using your hands. • Spread with the Gorgonzola and top with the onions. Sprinkle with the walnuts. • Bake for 15 minutes. Dot with the cream cheese and season with salt and pepper. Bake until the base is crisp and golden brown, 5–10 minutes. • Serve hot or at room temperature.

1 lb (500 g) pizza dough (see page 4)
8 oz (250 g) Gorgonzola cheese, at room temperature
1 tablespoon Worchestershire sauce
1 large white onion, thinly sliced
⅔ cup (100 g) walnuts
3 oz (90 g) cream cheese
Salt and freshly ground black pepper

33

SERVES 2–4
PREPARATION 40 min
RISING TIME about 1 h 30 min
COOKING 30 min
DIFFICULTY level 1

Pizza
with mushrooms

Prepare the pizza dough following the instructions on pages 4–5. Set aside to rise. • Preheat the oven to 425°F (220°C/gas 7). • Oil a 14-inch (35-cm) pizza pan. • Melt the butter in a large frying pan over medium heat. Add the garlic, mushrooms, and a pinch of salt. Sauté until the mushrooms are tender, 5–7 minutes. Remove from the heat. Remove and discard the garlic. • Knead the risen pizza dough briefly on a lightly floured work surface then press it into the prepared pan using your hands. • Spread with the tomatoes and top with the mushrooms. Add the Parmesan. Season with salt and pepper. Drizzle with the oil and bake until the crust is crisp and golden brown, 20–25 minutes. • Sprinkle with parsley and serve hot or at room temperature.

1 lb (500 g) pizza dough (see page 4)
2 tablespoons butter
1 clove garlic, lightly crushed but whole
12 oz (350 g) button mushrooms, sliced
Salt
1 (14-oz/400-g) can tomatoes, drained and chopped
1/3 cup (50 g) freshly grated Parmesan cheese
Freshly ground black pepper
2 tablespoons extra-virgin olive oil
1 tablespoon finely chopped parsley

SERVES 2–4
PREPARATION 30 min
RISING TIME about 1 h 30 min
COOKING 20–25 min
DIFFICULTY level 2

Seafood Pizza

Prepare the pizza dough following the instructions on pages 4–5. Set aside to rise. • Soak the mussels in cold water for 1 hour. Rinse and pull or scrub off any beards. • Preheat the oven to 425°F (220°C/gas 7). • Oil a 12-inch (30-cm) pizza pan. • Place the mussels in a large frying pan over high heat. Cook until they open, 5–7 minutes. Remove from the heat. • Shell the mussels, discarding any that did not open. • Heat 2 tablespoons of the oil in the same frying and sauté half the garlic until pale gold, 2–3 minutes. Add the mixed seafood and sauté over high heat for 5 minutes. • Knead the risen pizza dough briefly on a lightly floured work surface then press it into the prepared pan using your hands. • Spread with the tomatoes and sprinkle with the remaining garlic. • Drizzle the pizza with the reserved oil and season with salt and pepper. • Bake for 15 minutes. Remove from the oven and top with the mixed seafood and mussels. Bake until the seafood is cooked and the base is crisp and golden brown, 5–10 minutes. • Serve hot.

8 oz (250 g) mussels in shell
1 lb (500 g) pizza dough (see page 4)
¼ cup (60 ml) extra-virgin olive oil
6 cloves garlic, finely chopped
12 oz (350 g) mixed frozen seafood, thawed
Salt
1 (14-oz/400-g) can tomatoes, chopped, with juice
Freshly ground black pepper

SERVES 2–4
PREPARATION 30 min
RISING TIME about 2 h
COOKING 30–35 min
DIFFICULTY level 2

Filled Pizza
with mozzarella and tomatoes

Cook the eggs in a small saucepan over medium heat for 7 minutes from the moment the water reaches a boil. Drain and cool under cold running water. Shell and cut into wedges. • Cook the potatoes in a large pot of salted boiling water until tender, about 25 minutes. Drain well and mash until smooth. • Dissolve the yeast in the warm water. • Place the flour and salt in a large bowl. Add the yeast mixture, potatoes, and oil. Mix well with a wooden spoon to make a firm dough. • Knead the dough on a lightly floured work surface until smooth and elastic, 10–15 minutes. Let rise until doubled in volume, about 1 hour 30 minutes. • Roll out two-thirds of the dough on a lightly floured surface and then press it into the base and sides of an oiled 11 inch (28 cm) baking pan using your hands. • Place the mozzarella, eggs, tomatoes, and basil on top. Season with salt and pepper. Roll out the remaining dough and cover the pizza with it. Pinch around the edges to seal. • Cover and let rise for 30 minutes.• Preheat the oven to 425°F (220°C/gas 7). • Bake until the pizza is golden brown, 30–35 minutes. • Slice and serve hot.

2 large eggs

4 large potatoes, peeled

1 oz (30 g) fresh yeast or 2 ($1/4$-oz/7-g) packages active dry yeast

$1/4$ cup (60 ml) warm water

$2^2/3$ cups (400 g) all-purpose (plain) flour

Salt

2 tablespoons extra-virgin olive oil

5 oz (150 g) fresh mozzarella cheese, drained and sliced

20 cherry tomatoes, sliced

4–6 leaves fresh basil

Freshly ground black pepper

Pizza

with tomatoes and black olives

Prepare the pizza dough following the instructions on pages 4–5. Set aside to rise. • Preheat the oven to 425°F (220°C/gas 7). • Oil a 12-inch (30-cm) pizza pan. • Heat half the oil in a frying pan over medium heat. Add the onion and sauté until transparent, 3–4 minutes. Remove from the heat. • Knead the risen pizza dough briefly on a lightly floured work surface then press it into the prepared pan using your hands. • Spread with the tomatoes and top with the onion, capers, olives, and Pecorino. Season with salt and pepper and drizzle with the remaining oil. • Bake until the base is crisp and golden brown, 20–25 minutes. • Serve hot or at room temperature.

1 lb (500 g) pizza dough (see page 4)
1/3 cup (90 ml) extra-virgin olive oil
1 large onion, finely sliced
1 (14-oz/400-g) can tomatoes, chopped, with juice
1 tablespoon capers preserved in brine, drained and chopped
1 cup (100 g) black olives, pitted
4 oz (125 g) freshly grated Pecorino cheese
Salt and freshly ground black pepper

SERVES 2–4
PREPARATION 30 min
RISING TIME about 2 h 30 min
COOKING 20–25 min
DIFFICULTY level 1

Brown Pizza
with garlic

Prepare the whole-wheat pizza dough using the ingredients listed here and following the instructions on pages 4–5. Set aside to rise for 2 hours (If liked, make the dough using half whole-wheat flour and half all-purpose (plain) flour. The pizza will be a little lighter than when made with all whole-wheat flour). • Oil a 12-inch (30-cm) pizza pan. • Knead the risen pizza dough briefly on a lightly floured work surface then press it into the prepared pan using your hands. • Let rise for 30 minutes. • Preheat the oven to 425°F (220°C/gas 7). • Spread the dough with the tomatoes and sprinkle with the garlic. Drizzle with 2 tablespoons of the oil and season with salt and pepper • Bake for 15 minutes. Top with the mozzarella and bake until it is melted and the base is crisp and brown. • Drizzle with the remaining oil and serve hot.

Whole-Wheat Pizza Dough
$2^{2}/_{3}$ cups (400 g) whole-wheat (wholemeal) flour
Salt
1 oz (30 g) fresh yeast or 2($1/_4$-oz/7-g) packages active dry yeast
About $1/_2$ cup (125 ml) lukewarm water
2 tablespoons extra-virgin olive oil

Topping
1 (14-oz/400-g) can tomatoes, chopped, with juice
6 cloves garlic, coarsely chopped
$1/_4$ cup (60 ml) extra-virgin olive oil
Salt and freshly ground black pepper
5 oz (150 g) fresh mozzarella cheese, drained and cut into small cubes

SERVES 2–4
PREPARATION 30 min
RISING TIME about 1 h 30 min
COOKING 20–25 min
DIFFICULTY level 1

Pizza
with ham and mussels

Prepare the pizza dough following the instructions on pages 4–5. Set aside to rise. • Soak the mussels in a large bowl of cold water for 1 hour. Rinse well and pull or scrub of any beards. • Preheat the oven to 425°F (220°C/gas 7). • Oil a 12-inch (30-cm) pizza pan. • Place the mussels in a large saucepan over high heat. Cook until they open, 5–7 minutes. Shell the mussels, discarding any that did not open. • Heat half the oil in a large frying pan over medium heat. Add the mushrooms and sauté until tender, 5–7 minutes. • Knead the risen pizza dough briefly on a lightly floured work surface then press it into the prepared pan using your hands. • Spread the dough with the tomatoes. • Cover a quarter of the pizza with the mushrooms, a quarter with the ham, and a quarter with the mussels. Season with salt and pepper. Drizzle with the remaining oil. • Bake for 15 minutes. Sprinkle with the mozzarella. Bake until the base is crisp and golden brown and the cheese is melted, 5–10 minutes. • Serve hot.

8 oz (250 g) mussels in shell
1 lb (500 g) pizza dough (see page 4)
$\frac{1}{4}$ cup (60 ml) extra-virgin olive oil
8 oz (250 g) button mushrooms, sliced
1 cup (250 g) canned tomatoes, drained
3 oz (90 g) ham, cut into small cubes
Salt and freshly ground black pepper
4 oz (125 g) fresh mozzarella cheese, drained and sliced

SERVES 2–4
PREPARATION 30 min
RISING TIME about 1 h 30 min
COOKING 20–25 min
DIFFICULTY level 1

Neapolitan Pizza

Prepare the pizza dough following the instructions on pages 4–5. Set aside to rise. • Preheat the oven to 425°F (220°C/gas 7). • Oil a 12-inch (30-cm) pizza pan. • Knead the risen pizza dough briefly on a lightly floured work surface then press it into the prepared pan using your hands. • Spread with the the tomatoes. Add the anchovies and season with salt and pepper. Drizzle with the oil and sprinkle with oregano. Bake for 15 minutes. Top with the mozzarella and bake until the base is crisp and golden brown and the mozzarella is melted, 5–10 minutes. • Serve hot or at room temperature.

1 lb (500 g) pizza dough (see page 4)
1 (14-oz/400-g) can tomatoes, chopped, with juice
5 oz (150 g) fresh mozzarella cheese, drained and sliced
4–6 anchovy fillets, coarsely chopped
Salt and freshly ground black pepper
1/4 cup (60 ml) extra-virgin olive oil
1/2 teaspoon dried oregano

SERVES 2–4
PREPARATION 30 min
RISING TIME about 2 h
COOKING 20–25 min
DIFFICULTY level 1

Pizza
with sun-dried tomatoes

Prepare the pizza dough following the instructions on pages 4–5, incorporating 2 tablespoons of the oil into the dough as you work. Set aside to rise for 2 hours. • Preheat the oven to 425°F (220°C/gas 7). • Oil a 12-inch (30-cm) pizza pan. • Heat ¼ cup (60 ml) of the oil in a large frying pan over medium heat. Add the eggplants and sauté until tender, about 10 minutes. Place on a layer of paper towels using a slotted spoon and let drain. • Knead the risen pizza dough briefly on a lightly floured work surface then press it into the prepared pan using your hands. • Arrange the eggplant, tomatoes, and ham on the dough. Drizzle with the remaining oil and season with salt. Sprinkle with the thyme. • Bake until the base is crisp and golden brown, 20–25 minutes. • Garnish with the basil and serve hot or at room temperature.

1 lb (500 g) pizza dough (see page 4)
Salt
½ cup (125 ml) extra-virgin olive oil
2 medium eggplants (aubergines), sliced
3 oz (90 g) sun-dried tomatoes, soaked in warm water for 20 minutes, drained and coarsely chopped
2 oz (60 g) ham, chopped
1 teaspoon finely chopped thyme
1 sprig fresh basil, to garnish

SERVES 2–4
PREPARATION 30 min
RISING TIME about 1 h 30 min
COOKING 20–25 min
DIFFICULTY level 1

Pizza
with gorgonzola and pineapple

Prepare the pizza dough following the instructions on pages 4–5. Set aside to rise. • Preheat the oven to 425°F (220°C/gas 7). • Oil a 12-inch (30-cm) pizza pan. • Knead the risen pizza dough briefly on a lightly floured work surface then press it into the prepared pan using your hands. • Top with the mozzarella, Gorgonzola, garlic, and pineapple. Drizzle with oil and season with salt and pepper. • Bake until the base is crisp and golden brown, 20–25 minutes. • Serve hot or at room temperature.

1 lb (500 g) pizza dough (see page 4)
5 oz (150 g) fresh mozzarella cheese, drained and cut into small cubes
4 oz (125 g) Gorgonzola cheese, cut into small cubes
3 cloves garlic, finely sliced
5 oz (150 g) canned pineapple pieces, drained
2 tablespoons extra-virgin olive oil
Salt and freshly ground black pepper

SERVES 2–4
PREPARATION 30 min
RISING TIME about 1 h 30 min
COOKING 20–25 min
DIFFICULTY level 1

Pizza
with ham and mushrooms

Prepare the pizza dough following the instructions on pages 4–5. Set aside to rise. • Preheat the oven to 425°F (220°C/gas 7). • Oil a 12-inch (30-cm) pizza pan. • Knead the risen pizza dough briefly on a lightly floured work surface then press it into the prepared pan using your hands. • Spread with the tomatoes, ham, and mushrooms. Season with salt and pepper. Drizzle with the oil. • Bake for 15 minutes. Top with the mozzarella and bake until the cheese is melted and the base is crisp and golden brown, 5–10 minutes. • Serve hot or at room temperature.

1 lb (500 g) pizza dough (see page 4)
1 (14-oz/400-g) can tomatoes, chopped, with juice
4 oz (125 g) ham, chopped
12 mushrooms preserved in oil, quartered
Salt and freshly ground black pepper
2 tablespoons extra-virgin olive oil
5 oz (150 g) fresh mozzarella cheese, drained and sliced

SERVES 2–4
PREPARATION 30 min + 1 h to rest
RISING TIME about 1 h 30 min
COOKING 2 h 30 min
DIFFICULTY level 2

Pizza
with beef, zucchini, and eggplant

Prepare the pizza dough following the instructions on pages 4–5. Set aside to rise. • Oil a 12-inch (30-cm) pizza pan. • Place the zucchini and eggplant in a colander and sprinkle with salt. Let rest for 1 hour. • Heat half the oil in a large saucepan over medium heat. Add the onion, garlic, carrot, and celery and sauté until tender, about 5 minutes. • Add the beef and sauté until browned, about 5 minutes. • Add the wine and let it evaporate for 2 minutes. • Stir in the stock and tomato concentrate. Season with salt and pepper. Cover and cook over low heat for 2 hours. • Preheat the oven to 425°F (220°C/gas 7). • Rinse the zucchini and eggplant and drain well. • Heat the remaining oil in a large frying pan over medium heat. Cook the zucchini and the eggplant in small batches until tender, about 5 minutes per batch. • Knead the risen pizza dough briefly on a lightly floured work surface then press it into the prepared pan using your hands. • Arrange the zucchini and eggplant on top. Cover with the meat sauce. Bake until the base is crisp and golden brown, 20–25 minutes. Serve hot.

1 lb (500 g) pizza dough (see page 4)
2 medium zucchini (courgettes), thinly sliced lengthwise
1 large eggplant (aubergine), thinly sliced
12 oz (350 g) ground (minced) beef
Salt
½ cup (125 ml) extra-virgin olive oil
1 small onion, very finely chopped
1 clove garlic, very finely chopped
1 small carrot, very finely chopped
1 celery stick, very finely chopped
½ cup (125 ml) dry white wine
⅔ cup (150 ml) beef stock
2 tablespoons tomato concentrate (paste)
Freshly ground black pepper

SERVES 2–4
PREPARATION 30 min
RISING TIME about 1 h 30 min
COOKING 25–30 min
DIFFICULTY level 1

Cheese Pizza

with onion and apple

Prepare the pizza dough following the instructions on pages 4–5. Set aside to rise. • Preheat the oven to 400°F (200°C/gas 6). • Oil an 8 x 12-inch (20 x 30-cm) rectangular baking pan. • Melt the butter in a large frying pan over medium heat. Add the onions and garlic and sauté until softened, about 5 minutes. • Add the brandy and sauté until the brandy has evaporated, about 5 minutes. • Stir in the cream and simmer for 2 minutes. Season with salt and pepper and remove from the heat. • Thinly slice the apples and brush with the lemon juice. • Knead the risen pizza dough briefly on a lightly floured work surface then press it into the prepared pan using your hands. • Spread the onion mixture over the dough. Top with the Fontina, mozzarella, and apples. Season with salt and decorate with walnuts. • Bake until the base is crisp and golden brown and the topping is lightly browned, 25–30 minutes. • Serve hot.

1 lb (500 g) pizza dough (see page 4)
1/4 cup (60 g) butter
2 large onions, sliced
2 cloves garlic, thinly sliced
1/4 cup (60 ml) brandy
1/4 cup (60 ml) heavy (double) cream
Salt and freshly ground black pepper
2 large Granny Smith or other tart apples, peeled and cored
Juice of 1/2 lemon
5 oz (150 g) Fontina or other mild firm cheese, thinly sliced
4 oz (125 g) fresh mozzarella cheese, drained and cut into small cubes
8 walnuts, halved

SERVES 2–4
PREPARATION 30 min
RISING TIME about 1 h 30 min
COOKING 20–25 min
DIFFICULTY level 1

Cheese Pizza
with ham and mushrooms

Prepare the pizza dough following the instructions on pages 4–5. Set aside to rise. • Preheat the oven to 425°F (220°C/gas 7). • Oil a 12-inch (30-cm) pizza pan. • Place the tomatoes in a medium bowl and season with salt and pepper. Add 2 tablespoons of oil and mix well. • Heat the remaining oil in a large frying pan over medium heat. Add the mushrooms and garlic, and sauté until the mushrooms are tender and most of the cooking juices have evaporated, 6–8 minutes. • Remove from the heat. Remove and discard the garlic. • Knead the risen pizza dough briefly on a lightly floured work surface then press it into the prepared pan using your hands. • Spread with the tomato mixture. Top with the ham, mushrooms, mozzarella, and Gorgonzola. • Bake until the base is crisp and golden brown, 20–25 minutes. • Sprinkle with oregano and serve hot.

1 lb (500 g) pizza dough (see page 4)
1 (14-oz/400-g) can tomatoes, chopped, with juice
Salt and freshly ground black pepper
1/4 cup (60 ml) extra-virgin olive oil
10 oz (300 g) white mushrooms, sliced
1 clove garlic, lightly crushed but whole
4 oz (125 g) ham, chopped
5 oz (150 g) fresh mozzarella cheese, drained and cut into small cubes
4 oz (125 g) Gorgonzola, cut into small cubes
1 teaspoon dried oregano

SERVES 2–4
PREPARATION 30 min
RISING TIME about 1 h 30 min
COOKING 20–25 min
DIFFICULTY level 1

Pizza
with garlic, ham, and artichokes

Prepare the pizza dough following the instructions on pages 4–5. Set aside to rise. • Preheat the oven to 425°F (220°C/gas 7). • Oil a 12-inch (30-cm) pizza pan. • Knead the risen pizza dough briefly on a lightly floured work surface then press it into the prepared pan using your hands. • Spread with the tomatoes and sprinkle with the garlic. Top with the artichokes, ham, and olives. Season with salt and pepper. • Bake for 15 minutes. Top with the mozzarella and drizzle with the oil. Bake until the base is crisp and golden brown and the mozzarella is melted, 5–10 minutes. • Sprinkle with the parsley and serve hot.

1 lb (500 g) pizza dough (see page 4)
1 (14-oz/400-g) can tomatoes, chopped, with juice
1 clove garlic, very finely sliced
10 artichoke hearts, preserved in oil, cut into segments
4 oz (125 g) ham, chopped
10 black olives, pitted
Salt and freshly ground black pepper
5 oz (150 g) fresh mozzarella cheese, drained and sliced
1/4 cup (60 ml) extra-virgin olive oil
1 tablespoon finely chopped parsley

SERVES 2–4
PREPARATION 30 min
RISING TIME about 1 h 30 min
COOKING 1 h 5–10 min
DIFFICULTY level 1

Pizza
with potatoes and pancetta

Prepare the pizza dough following the instructions on pages 4–5. Set aside to rise. • Preheat the oven to 400°F (200°C/gas 6). • Oil a 12-inch (30-cm) pizza pan. • Heat the oil in a roasting pan over medium heat. Add the rosemary and the thyme. Add the potatoes, season with salt, and mix well. Bake until the potatoes are tender and golden brown, 40–45 minutes. Remove from the oven and let cool slightly. • Increase the oven temperature to 425°F (220°C/gas 7.) • Knead the risen pizza dough briefly on a lightly floured work surface then press it into the prepared pan using your hands. • Arrange the pancetta, mozzarella, and potatoes on top. • Bake for 15 minutes. Remove from the oven and sprinkle with the mozzarella.
Bake until the pizza is crisp and golden brown.,
5–10 minutes. • Serve hot.

1 lb (500 g) pizza dough (see page 4)
⅓ cup (90 ml) extra-virgin olive oil
Sprig of rosemary
Sprig of thyme
10 oz (300 g) potatoes,
    peeled and cut into small cubes
Salt
3 oz (90 g) pancetta (or bacon),
    cut into small cubes
5 oz (150 g) fresh mozzarella cheese,
    drained and sliced thinly

SERVES 2–4
PREPARATION 30 min
RISING TIME about 2 h 30 min
COOKING 20–25 min
DIFFICULTY level 1

Brown Pizza
with three-cheese topping

Prepare the whole-wheat pizza dough using the ingredients listed here and following the instructions on pages 4–5. Set aside to rise for 2 hours. • Oil a 12-inch (30-cm) pizza pan.• Knead the risen pizza dough briefly on a lightly floured work surface then press it into the prepared pan using your hands. • Let rise for another 30 minutes. • Preheat the oven to 425°F (220°C/gas 7). • Three-Cheese Topping: Beat together the oil and milk in a small bowl. Brush the dough with this mixture. • Top with alternate layers of the three cheeses. Season with salt and pepper. • Bake until the cheeses are melted and bubbling and the base is crisp and golden brown, 20–25 minutes. • Garnish with the oregano and serve hot.

Pizza Dough
1⅓ cups (200 g) whole-wheat (wholemeal) flour
1⅓ cups (200 g) all-purpose (plain) flour
Salt
1 oz (30 g) fresh yeast or 2 (¼-oz/7-g) packages active dry yeast
About ½ cup (125 ml) lukewarm water
2 tablespoons extra virgin olive oil

Three-Cheese Topping
2 tablespoons extra virgin olive oil
2 tablespoons milk
4 oz (125 g) Fontina or other mild firm cheese, thinly sliced
4 oz (125 g) Gorgonzola cheese, thinly sliced
4 oz (125 g) fresh mozzarella cheese, drained and thinly sliced
Freshly ground black pepper
1 tablespoon finely chopped oregano

SERVES 2–4
PREPARATION 30 min
RISING TIME about 1 h 30 min
COOKING 20–25 min
DIFFICULTY level 1

Pizza
with zucchini flowers

Prepare the pizza dough following the instructions on pages 4–5. Set aside to rise. • Preheat the oven to 425°F (220°C/gas 7). • Oil a 14-inch (35-cm) pizza pan. • Knead the risen pizza dough briefly on a lightly floured work surface then press it into the prepared pan using your hands. • Drizzle with half the oil and cover with the mozzarella. • Bake for 15 minutes. Top with the zucchini flowers and cherry tomatoes and drizzle with the remaining oil. Bake until he base is crisp and golden brown, 5–10 minutes. • Serve hot or at room temperature.

1 lb (500 g) pizza dough (see page 4)
2 tablespoons extra-virgin olive oil
6 oz (180 g) water buffalo mozzarella cheese, thinly sliced
4–6 large zucchini flowers, rinsed and dried
10–12 cherry tomatoes, cut in half
Salt and freshly ground black or white pepper

Calzone
with mushrooms and tomatoes

Prepare the pizza dough following the instructions on pages 4–5. Set aside to rise. • Preheat the oven to 425°F (220°C/gas 7). • Oil a large baking sheet. • Heat the oil in a large frying pan over medium heat. Add the mushrooms and garlic and sauté until the mushrooms are tender and most of the cooking juices have evaporated, 7–10 minutes. • Stir in the parsley and season with salt. Remove from the heat. Remove and discard the garlic. • Divide the dough into two equal portions. Roll out into $1/8$-inch (3-mm) thick disks. Place one on the prepared baking sheet. • Spread half the disk with half the tomatoes leaving $3/4$ inch (2 cm) free around the edges. Add half the mozzarella and mushrooms. Sprinkle with half the Parmesan. Fold the dough over the filling and seal the edges, pinching them together firmly. Repeat with the other disk. • Bake until the dough is crisp and golden brown, about 30 minutes. • Serve hot.

1 lb (500 g) pizza dough (see page 4)
2 tablespoons extra-virgin olive oil
12 oz (350 g) white mushrooms, sliced
1 clove garlic, lightly crushed but whole
1 tablespoon finely chopped parsley
Salt
1 (14-oz/400-g) can tomatoes, chopped, with juice
4 oz (125 g) fresh mozzarella cheese, drained and cut into small cubes
$1/2$ cup (50 g) freshly grated Parmesan

Calzone
with spinach and mushrooms

Prepare the pizza dough following the instructions on pages 4–5. Set aside to rise. • Preheat the oven to 425°F (220°C/gas 7). • Oil a large baking sheet. • Heat the oil in a large frying pan over medium heat. Add the mushrooms and garlic and sauté until the mushrooms are tender, 7–10 minutes. • Stir in the parsley and season with salt. Remove from the heat. • Heat the remaining oil in the same pan over medium heat. Add the spinach and capers, and sauté for 2–3 minutes. • Divide the dough into two equal portions. Roll out into $\frac{1}{8}$-inch (3-mm) thick disks. Place one on the prepared baking sheet. • Spread half the disk with half the tomatoes leaving $\frac{3}{4}$ inch (2 cm) free around the edges. • Add half the ricotta, mushrooms, and spinach. Sprinkle with half the Parmesan. • Fold the dough over the filling and seal the edges, pinching together firmly. Repeat with the other disk. • Bake until the dough is crisp and golden brown, about 30 minutes. • Serve hot.

1 lb (500 g) pizza dough (see page 4)
$\frac{1}{4}$ cup (60 ml) extra-virgin olive oil
5 oz (150 g) white mushrooms, sliced
1 clove garlic, finely chopped
1 tablespoon finely chopped parsley
Salt
8 oz (250 g) cooked spinach, drained
1 tablespoon capers, rinsed
1 (14-oz/400-g) can tomatoes, drained and chopped
6 oz (180 g) ricotta cheese, drained
$\frac{1}{2}$ cup (50 g) freshly grated Parmesan

Index

Copyright © 2007 by McRae Books Srl

This English edition first published in 2007

Pizza

was created and produced by McRae Books Srl

Borgo Santa Croce, 8 – Florence (Italy)

info@mcraebooks.com

Publishers: Anne McRae and Marco Nardi

Project Director: Anne McRae

Design: Sara Mathews

Text: Carla Bardi

Editing: Osla Fraser

Photography: Cristina Canepari, Keeho Casati, Gil Gallo, Walter Mericchi, Sandra Preussinger

Home Economist: Benedetto Rillo

Artbuying: McRae Books

Layouts: Adina Stefania Dragomir

Repro: Fotolito Raf, Florence

ISBN 978-88-89272-91-6

Printed and bound in China